# Poems I forgot

Mark James

Presentation by *BookLeaf Publishing*

Web: www.bookleafpub.com

E-mail: info@bookleafpub.com

ISBN: 9789358369700

First edition 2022

# Working Title

What I am doing feels like an insult to the
written word.
After all, sage words of wisdom echo, keep
polishing the turd.
Maintain the heat and pressure, you'll eventually
get a diamond.
Precious gems seem an arrogant goal, as those
before me, I doubt I'm destined
There is a less personal wisdom, this one about
potters
A vessel is a much nicer descriptor
Humility also begotten here
Create two groups
one making lots, dumbly
the other seeking quality
Hands working numbly begot more fine pieces
than hands working self assuredly.

# Church

Worship is not for me, I prefer to commune with nature
Acknowledging your beauty and perfection does not bring me closer to the divine
Only in the quiet serenity of nature do I find the sublime
Where your curves make me think I am touching something greater
Touching nature's curves brings me towards the creator
Walls, furnishings and momentary ecstasy you may claim
Open spaces full of harmony are where I actually feel sane

# La Push

Treacherous, slippery footing
Heart rate, astounding
A light walk in the woods
Unexpectedly a sharp escarpment
away from the drop you are shying
duplicitous beauty I'm ignoring
alighting a cliff face are our moods
securely, feet setting
a hand for you reaching
momentarily my ego gets a dent
taking my hand you toss off your hood
happy rollers crashing
on a log contentedly resting
both of us for this glorious moment
worlds end at the bottom of a cliff in the wood

# No difference

Far away she sent me
All ties severed from we
never giving up the ship
i fought on, firing from the hip
My world burned, she said I was the culprit
spraying everything with napalm from her pulpit
Look what you have done she cries
chasing me away from my children's eyes
Continuing to pay the bills, do therapy, sacrifice,
I hear what a monster I am
A year goes like this until a motorcycle crash
shakes things up
Her opinions changed after I was almost ketchup
After all this time, she claimed it was all fine,
she cannot stand me moving forward, to her it
crosses a line
its the thing she desired
for me moving on seemed a dreadful quagmire
Now that I am, I'm in more trouble
you hate me and I'm awful she blubbers
giving her what she never did, I tell her she is
actually quite splendid
Her feelings make no sense, and everything I do
makes no difference

# +5 STR

Quiet endurance
overt humility
casual selflessness
that is strength

dedicated service
willing self sacrifice
steadfast loyalty
that is strength

# Oops

Distraction for the distressed resident
performing impromptu disimpaction
ironically the remedy was prickly pear jalapeno
jam

It was no ordinary malady like constipation
giving us such consternation
rather it was a gunshot victim

I don't want surgery I just want to thug it out
no one likes when the Darwin award winner
starts to pout

News for you my dude, drop the attitude,
hard to thug it out when you got shot in the place
your poop comes out

# A little Crazy

You have to be crazy to do what I do
not the motorcycle thing, that is an act of
confidence
    traffic is simply one big dance
not parenting, that is an act of love,
    gentle like a dove
not nursing, that is sheer dedication,
    illness takes no vacation
writing, writing is different,
    every day you must pay the rent
create entire worlds, but don't hide in them
    share, sell, and mind the lyric hem
believe in yourself, and trust others can see
    to me that is what is truly crazy

# Mornings

Rolling over I feel her warmth, but she isn't
placidly emerging from a deep and restful
slumber.
Awkwardly I lumber to her, she is wide awake
and doing, I feel like a dolt for snoozing
Kissing and cuddling, she's happy to see me,
there's none of the resentment I have grown
accustomed to
New, this is absolutely new.
Coffee brought to me while I try to divine the
mental fog, a knowing smile on her lips.
Hips don't lie, and hers give a silent promise as
she walks away
Everything will be grand, if you just follow me
and start your day.

# Plastic

plastic figures are strewn haphazardly between
us, the meanings of their positions only clear to
the initiated
Several dozen figures in baroque armor, painted
with a loving attention to detail, bordering on
obsessive
dice clatter, curses from one, but not the other,
the fate of a soldier, a squad, an army, or a whole
world riding on the pips
Out come the rulers, the rule books and the
arguments
for a few minutes it is as tense as any first down
measurement
then some of the figures are removed, then
another roll of the dice, and more disappear from
the board.
trauma, anxiety and depression are fought
valiantly with little bits of plastic

# Grandfather

there once was a man who cut apples with a
pocket knife,
there was always butterscotch in the center
console of his car
sticks were never good enough, what I imagined,
he would craft
he cured hiccups with sugar on his finger, and
solved most problems with peanut butter
crackers
he never let on about being ill, he always
maintained a strong front
in the community he was known as a kind man
there are letters, and quirky presents, and all the
signs of love,
but i never really got to know him, for I was
taken far away, and no one told me what letters
really are.

# Letters

A single sheet of paper, covered in words, typed
or written,
something deeply personal, entirely inexpensive,
able to change the fate of the world
at least it used to be.
once, not so long ago, a letter was the ultimate I
love you
simply sending one shows that you are willing to
grant time and thought and energy
then the content
it can make you content
or it can completely unravel everything
but now they are robbed of the power
a letter is just a piece of paper
and its meaning is lost

# curing writer's block

curing writer's block is simple
just start writing
ignore your grand vision
set aside your pride
don't worry about all of the things you want to
express
it doesn't matter
the turmoil of your soul
the whirlpool of emotions that could birth epics
you can't get those things onto the page
first there is this block to deal with
chip away at it, one letter at a time
what comes out is not profound
this is not a crime
just get it out
move forward
gain a new perspective
the block is only temporary,
your spark is not

# fear is the problem

holding us back has always been the goal
what do you expect from a society that thrives
on husbandry
the Them want control
its human nature, find something stronger than
you and harness it
let that thing you tamed do what you need done
in the case of people it is rather easy
when people are afraid you do not even need to
raise the leather braid
and so many already have fear in the heart
fear of failure, fear of success, fear of instability,
fear of being just like the rest, or worse standing
out and losing the comfort of anonymous
mediocrity
so all They need is a little nudge
a spark to light the toxic sludge
so you see, it is very much a problem when
people are encouraged to live afraid

# In between

In between is where we all want to be
the magic there is magic we see
in between times
in between spaces
that magical precipice where anything is
possible
that place where every good thing is probable
that hopeful time before we cross the threshold
that minute before going over the precipice
we all just want to hold on to the promise
we felt when we were in between

# Fifteen

In a culture, not my own, you become a woman
when you turn fifteen
Though I cannot make a Tilde with these keys, it
is something I have seen
There is the typical awkward culture clash and
first dance feeling
but sometimes it is a spectacle that leaves you
reeling
Like when the adults get carried away with the
celebration
and no one wants to stop the fun
so the sober fourteen year old is chosen to drive
and is responsible for keeping the newly minted
woman alive
adult cousin in the back, pleas bring back a
twelve pack
A chivalrous child received a concussion, but
the Lord was less loving of the drunk this time
Transected is a fun term, it means the drunken
cousin was split in half by extreme forces
And what of the young lady for which all this
excitement was made
her abdomen was surgically filleted

She was on a bypass machine for several weeks,
while we sewed up her liver, and looked for
what was left of her spleen
fifteen years old, with at least fifteen surgeries,
needing probably fifteen years of therapy
A young woman's life destroyed by a poorly
executed tradition
but i guess at least she has one

# House of healing

One of those things happened, that aren't
supposed to happen
Don't worry, he says, it will all get lost in the
sauce, idly charting with a pen
last night a guest from the prison tried to inject
crushed up pills into his IV
needless to say he did not get to feel groovy
he passed, and you could say he also got sauced,
and will be lost in the sauce
a skeletal woman, so quiet and sweet, stands by
the nurses station
seeking acceptance and comfort at her
appearance, perhaps just wanting more
interaction
her nose and ears are gone from trying to
commit self immolation
she got to go home, her expectations exceeded
we heard a few days later at suicide she
succeeded
just another awful event to add to the sauce
then there was an old man, who refused to eat
food
fortunately he was roomed with a fellow of jolly
mood
If getting him to eat is what you need,

than grant this man our finest weed
Within hours his appetite returned,
and at least one persons candle continued to
burn
but this was also lost in the sauce
ventilated patients, encephalopathy patients,
terminal patients and criminal patients, old,
young, valid, and not
all of them just get lost in the sauce.

# Clutter

Life gets cluttered
it starts as soon as we're born
stuff and things, things and stuff
all get pushed towards us
it's all necessary and must be had

getting older our life is littered
with things spanning back to our life's morn
things and fluff
now it becomes outrageous
some of it is necessary, some frivolous, and
some bad

near the end we are often embittered
dividing our clutter, feeling our life being torn
afraid of hearing our loved ones guff
our efforts of retention now porous
give them the things, show them you loved them
by giving them everything you ever had

# Whiskey

I wanted to need her.
It was my goal to be so consumed by our love,
to be wholly unable to live without her.
Since she left me I have discovered,
I do not even want her.

# Last thought

From the day you become a father, you come
last in all things
At least that's what I used as an excuse to justify
my mistreatment
No matter how good I am
No matter how hard I try
No matter what I give out provide
The people I think have my best interests at
heart
Only care that I play their part
Whatever it is they want
If I fulfill that need, then maybe just maybe,
after all is said and done they will spare me a
thought

# Love yourself

No one was coming to rescue me
My world had been shattered, staying on the
floor was all that mattered
I was cared for, nobody could get to my door
the world at large was quarantined, and
responsibility had my loved ones detained
Reaching out to a stranger was the best thing I
could have done, it taught me that
　　it was fine to do the bare minimum
So I started with just showing up to work, and to
my delight I was able to focus
　　on patient care
Once my weekend arrived I got a wretched scare
I found myself in my room, with no desire to do
anything.
No one was coming to rescue me, and I knew I
had to do something
It took hours to get out of my room and go to the
store, but I did it.
Time passed, and the next weekend I went to the
park, it took hours to get out
　　of the door, but I did it.
Day in and day out, I rescued myself, learned
what my needs were, and I came
　　to love and forgive myself.

My world had shattered, but I had not, and in
that crucible I found love for myself.

# Poem 21

One poem a day for three weeks
Oh that is easy, this should be neat
Somehow it became five this day, none on that
Goals met, it's deadline night
Pick a picture, dedicate your book, ad a
forewarn
Foreward?
Forward!
Are you sure you want THAT picture?
Check your edits
Don't submit this, it's trash!
There is no such thing as bad art!
Rule one of poetry is there are no rules
Your prose, your verse, your words, they are
yours
For you
This was all to showcase what you can do
A catalyst, the seed crystal
whatever anyone takes from this
whether it sells like wildfire, or dies on the
editing floor
You finally wrote a love letter to yourself,
unashamedly
But are you sure you wanted that picture?